Hide and Seek:
Wild Animal Groups in North America

Written by Caroline Fernandez
Illustrated by Erin Mercer

DC Canada Education Publishing

Author: Caroline Fernandez

Illustrator: Erin Mercer

Editors: Kara Cybanski, Leonard Judge

Cover Design: Erin Mercer

Published in 2023 by: DC Canada Education Publishing

28 Concourse Gate, Unit 105
Ottawa, ON, Canada, K2E 7T7
www.dc-canada.ca

Funded by the
Government
of Canada | Canada

Hide and Seek: Wild Animal Groups in North America

ISBN: 978-1-77205-799-7

Library and Archives Canada Cataloguing in Publication

Title: Hide and seek : wild animal groups in North America / written by
Caroline Fernandez ;   illustrated by Erin Mercer.

Other titles: Wild animal groups in North America

Names: Fernandez, Caroline (Blogger), author. | Mercer, Erin, 1986- illustrator.

Identifiers: Canadiana 2022039881X | ISBN 978-1-77205-799-7

Subjects: LCSH: Picture puzzles—Juvenile literature. | LCSH: Animals—North America—
Juvenile

literature. | LCGFT: Picture puzzles.

Classification: LCC GV1507.P47 F47 2022 | DDC j793.73—dc23

Printed in China 2023

Dedication

For everyone who likes to find things in books.

~ Caroline Fernandez

This book is for those who love getting lost in the details.

~ Erin Mercer

Oh no, butterfly,
you don't fit here.
Did you get separated
from your group?

Do you belong in a pod?
A gaggle?
A bob?

Find out to which groups
the arctic wolf and
the arctic hare
belong...

A down of arctic hares
A pack of arctic wolves

Arctic hares have a white coat because it acts as camouflage in winter for protection against predators like wolves, polar bears, foxes, and owls.

Find this wolf, this hare, a butterfly. and the rock shaped like a hare.

Arctic wolves eat caribou, muskox, and arctic hares. They live in northern regions of North America and Greenland.

A celebration of polar bears
A huddle of walrus

Polar bears live in the Arctic and are strong swimmers. They generally feed on seals. Their fur is white but their skin is black.

Find this polar bear, this walrus, and a butterfly. Where is the polar bear's butt?

Walrus are large arctic mammals. They can live up to 40 years in the wild and have huge tusks.

Polar cod live in the freezing cold water of the Arctic. They are the food source for narwhals, seals, and beluga whales.

A lap of polar cod
A blessing of narwhals

Find this polar cod,
this narwhal,
and a butterfly.

Where is the piece of ice
being poked by a narwhal?

Narwhals are mammals that live in the Arctic. They are
known as "the unicorn of the sea" because of their tusks.

A herd of moose
An earth of red fox

Moose are large, herbivorous mammals that can live up to 15-20 years in the wild.

Find this moose, this
red fox, and a butterfly.

Where is the tree with antlers?

Red foxes are clever mammals. They generally hunt at night
and eat rabbits, mice, snakes, and berries.

A flock of Canada geese
A scurry of flying squirrels

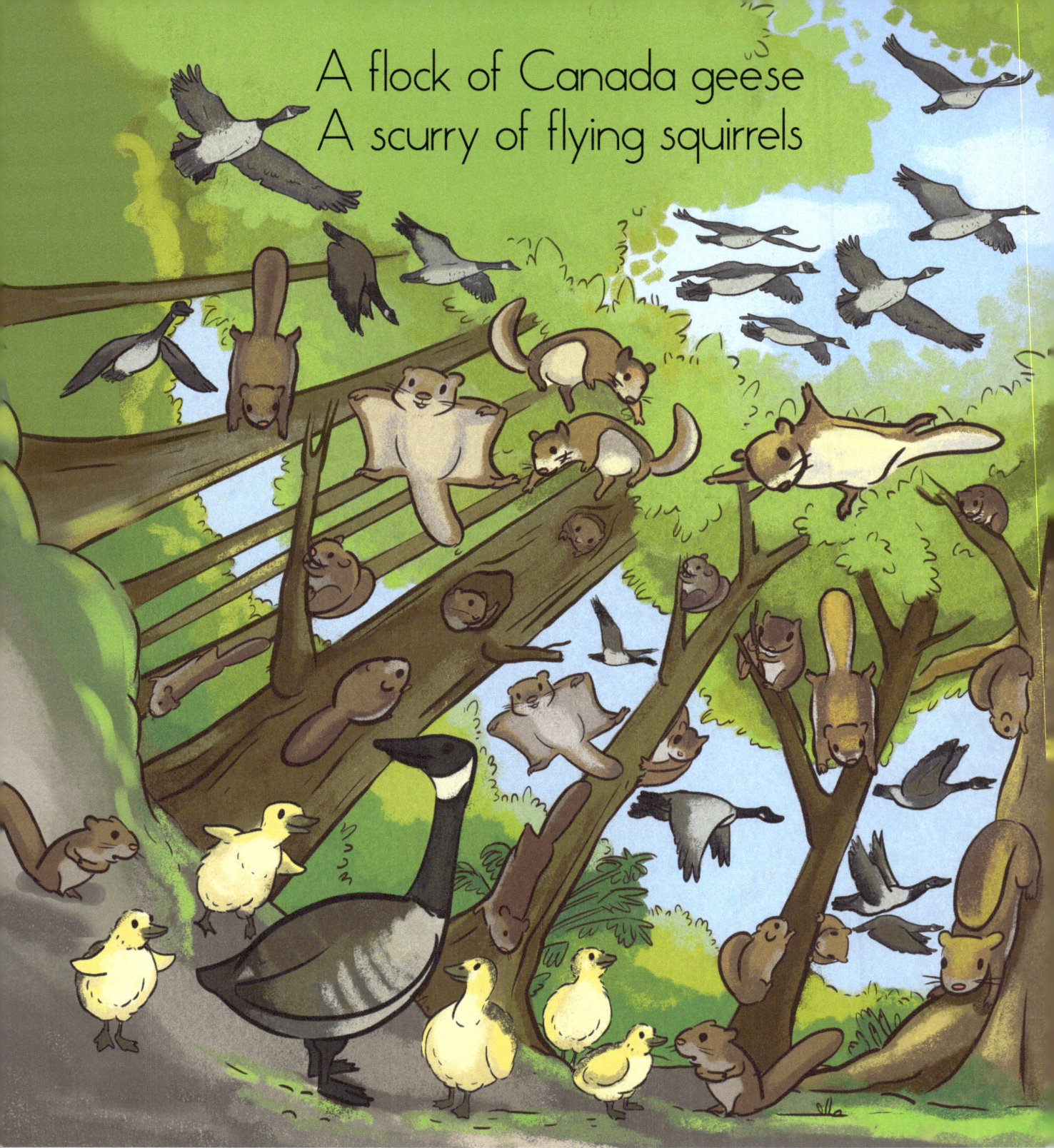

Canada geese graze on grass, grains, and berries.
They can live up to 24 years in the wild.

Find this goose,
this squirrel, and a butterfly.

Where is the goose flying
the wrong way?

There are more than 40 species of **flying squirrels** in the world. These squirrels don't actually fly, but glide from tree to tree — which looks like flying.

A gaze of raccoons
A parliament of snowy owls

Raccoons are nocturnal mammals that live all over the world. They walk on four paws.

Find this owl, this raccoon, and a butterfly.

Where is the fattest raccoon?

Snowy owls mainly live in the Arctic tundra. Males are generally whiter than females, which are brownish with dark markings.

A colony of beavers
A swarm of honey bees

Beavers can live up to 24 years. They are the largest rodents in North America and can be found in rivers, ponds, lakes, and wetlands, where they build dams.

Find this beaver, this bee, and a butterfly.

Where is the sleeping bee?

Honey bees are social creatures that live together in hives or nests. They produce the honey we eat and pollinate our flowers.

17

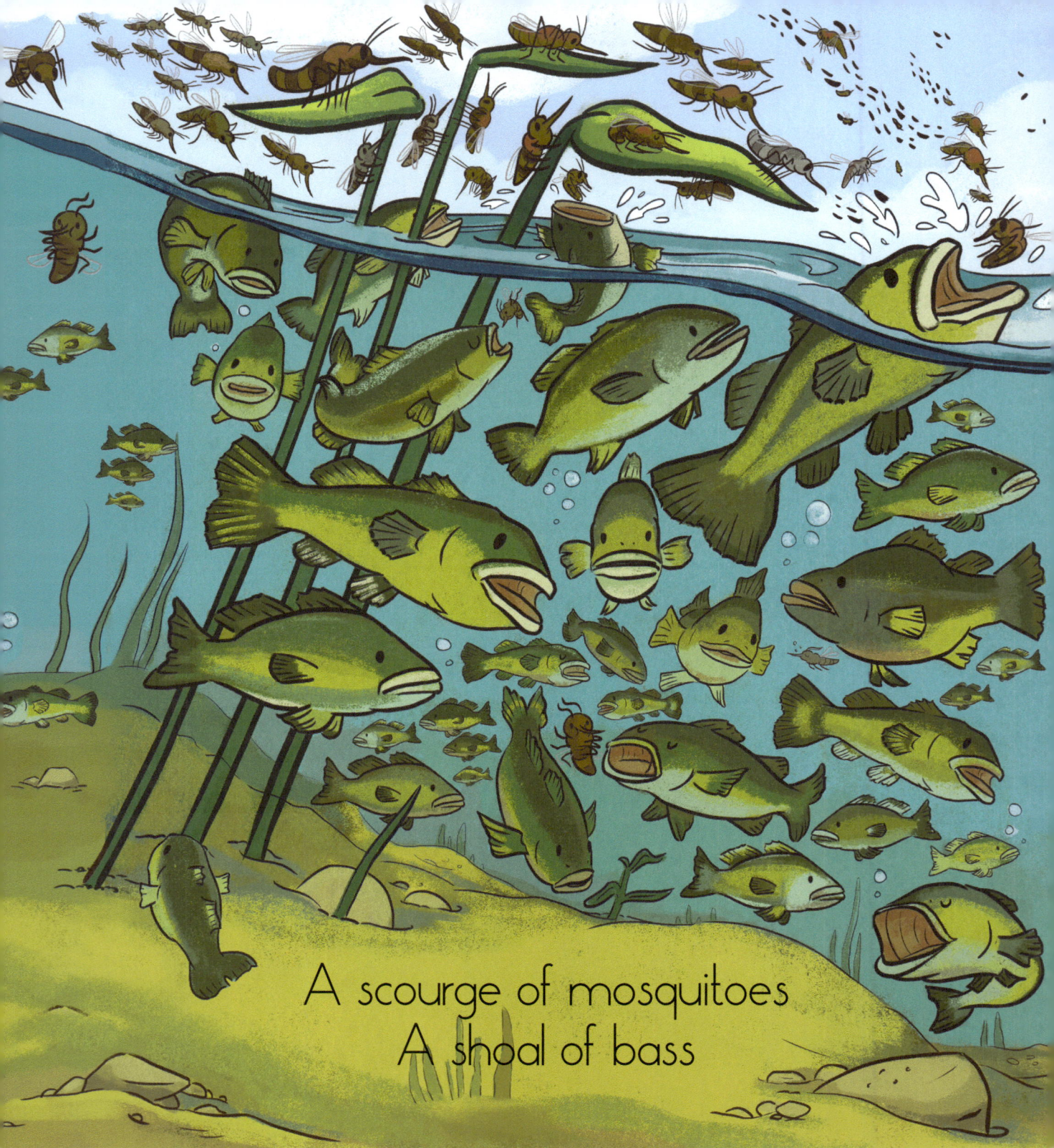

A scourge of mosquitoes
A shoal of bass

Only female **mosquitoes** bite humans and animals. Male mosquitoes feed on plants and only live for about a week.

Find this mosquito, this bass, and a butterfly.

Where are the seven underwater mosquitoes?

Bass are members of the sunfish family and live in fresh water.

A cloud of bats
A knot of toads

There are more than 1,300 species of **bats** on Earth. Some can live up to 30 years in the wild. The Bumblebee Bat is the smallest mammal (in length).

Find this bat,
this toad, and a butterfly.

Where is the toad on its back?

There are more than 300 different species of **toads** in the world. Toads have short legs compared to frogs.

A steam of minnows
A mischief of mice

Minnows are small freshwater fish found in North America.
They are usually silver and measure less than four inches.

Find this minnow, this mouse, and a butterfly.

Where are the two minnows talking to a mouse?

Mice are generally nocturnal rodents that have slender bodies and sharp claws.

Ponies are small horses that come in many colours. They are a good breed for children to ride.

A string of ponies
A kine of cows

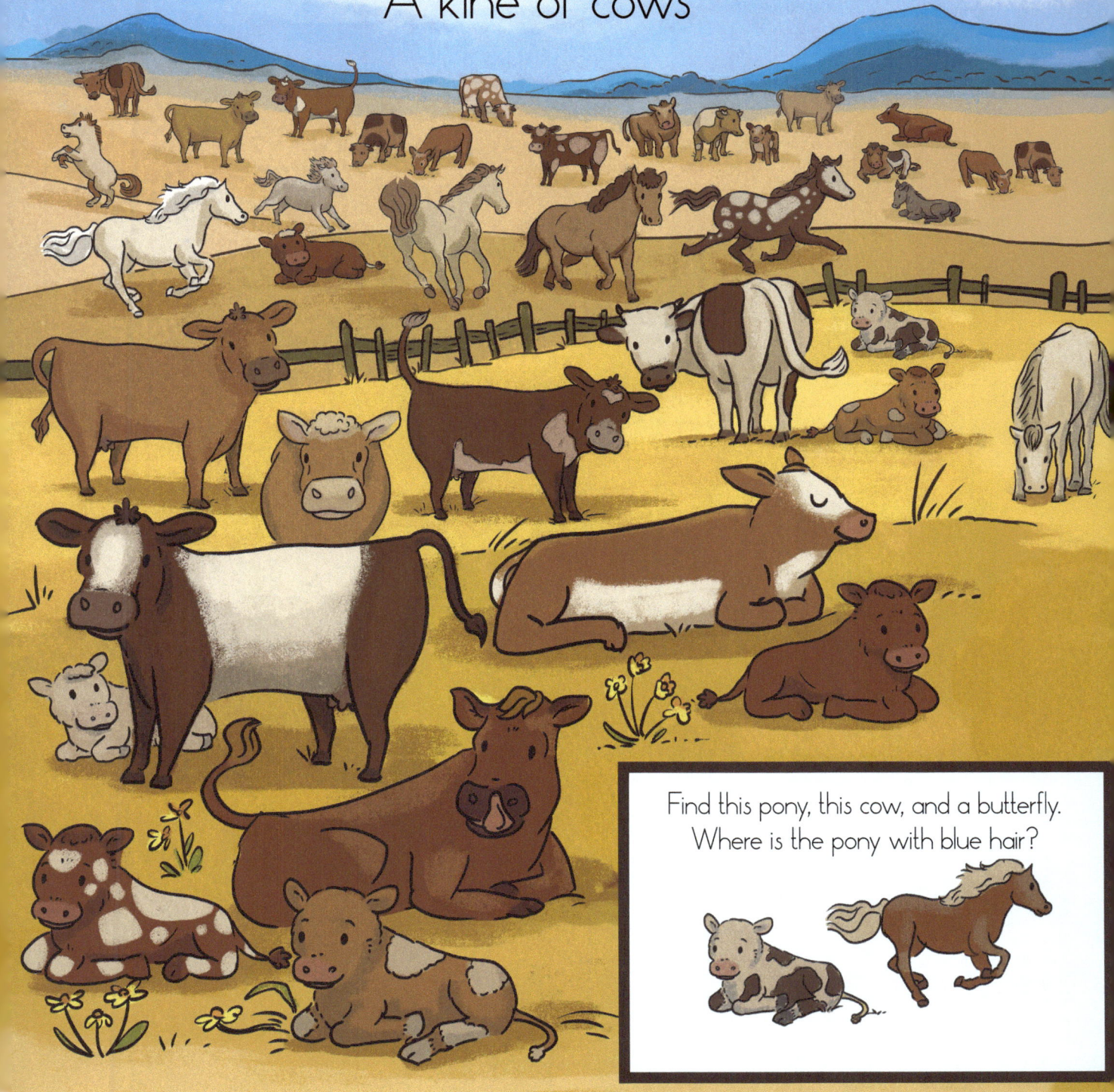

Find this pony, this cow, and a butterfly.
Where is the pony with blue hair?

Cows are the most common farm animal in the world. They are raised for dairy and meat products and come in many colours.

A cast of peregrine falcons
A run of salmon

Peregrine falcons can be found in the tundra, desert, mountains, and even in cities. These carnivores can live up to 17 years.

Find this falcon, this salmon, and a butterfly.

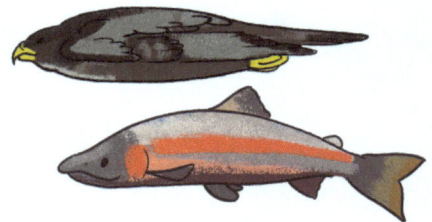

Where are the two worms?

Salmon can live in both salt water and fresh water. These fish travel long distances to return to the place they were born to spawn.

A pod of orcas
A bob of seals

Orcas hunt together in groups and feed on fish, seals, walrus, penguins, sharks, and even other species of whales. They can live up to 80 years.

Find this orca, this seal, and a butterfly.

Where is the brown orca asleep on a rock?

Seals are great swimmers and easily hunt for fish. They can live up to 20 years in the wild.

A flutter of butterflies

Each year, **Monarch butterflies** migrate from their home in Canada through the United States to Central Mexico - more than 3,200 kilometres.

Find this lost butterfly that is so happy to be back in its group!

What interesting facts do you know about the animals that live in your community?

Collective Nouns for Animals in This Book

What is a collective noun?

A collective noun is a singular noun that refers to a group, in this case a group of animals. You could see one arctic wolf... but if you see many arctic wolves, you would call them by their collective noun, a **pack** of wolves.

Why should we learn animal group names?

Though only some of these group names, like a pack of wolves and a flock of birds, are commonly used in English, expanding your vocabulary is a great way to challenge your brain and learn something new.

Which collective nouns had you heard before reading this book? Circle them.

- A pack of arctic wolves
- A down of arctic hares
- A celebration of polar bears
- A huddle of walrus
- A lap of polar cod
- A blessing of narwhals
- A herd of moose
- An earth of red fox
- A flock of Canada geese
- A scurry of flying squirrels
- A gaze of raccoons
- A parliament of snowy owls
- A colony of beavers
- A swarm of honey bees
- A scourge of mosquitoes
- A shoal of bass
- A cloud of bats
- A knot of toads
- A steam of minnows
- A mischief of mice
- A string of ponies
- A kine of cows
- A cast of peregrine falcons
- A run of salmon
- A pod of orcas
- A bob of seals
- A flutter of butterflies

Other Collective Nouns for Animals

There are many other animal groups whose names are not in this book. Here are a few. Which others do you know?

- A colony or an army of ants
- A brood of chickens
- A pod of dolphins
- A memory of elephants
- A cackle of hyenas
- A descent of woodpeckers
- An ambush of tigers
- A school of fish
- A caravan of camels
- A herd of elk

- _____
- _____
- _____
- _____
- _____
- _____
- _____
- _____
- _____
- _____

Where do we get the names for these animal groups?

There isn't one specific person who decides what we should call animal groups. The English language evolves over time and common usage of a term often determines if it will be considered correct.

Some words are used for more than one type of animal. A swarm is usually a group of insects, a herd is usually for animals like horses and deer, and a pod is usually for sea mammals like dolphins and orcas. But there is no real rule for which animal groups are called by which names.

Imagine you had to come up with an animal group name. What would it be and for which animals?

About the Animals

A

ARCTIC HARE - A down of arctic hares
The arctic hare's coat is white because it acts as camouflage in winter for protection against predators like wolves, polar bears, foxes, and owls.

ARCTIC WOLF - A pack of arctic wolves
Arctic wolves eat caribou, muskox, and arctic hares. They live in northern regions of North America and Greenland.

B

BASS - A shoal of bass
Bass are members of the sunfish family and live in fresh water.

BAT - A cloud of bats
There are more than 1,300 species of bats on Earth. Some can live up to 30 years in the wild. The Bumblebee Bat is the smallest species of bat and the smallest mammal (in length).

BEAVER - A colony of beavers
Beavers can live up to 24 years. They are the largest rodents in North America and can be found in rivers, ponds, lakes, and wetlands, where they build dams.

BUTTERFLY - A flutter of butterflies
Each year, Monarch butterflies migrate from their home in Canada through the United States to Central Mexico - more than 3,200 kilometres.

C

CANADA GOOSE - A flock of Canada geese
Canada geese graze on grass, grains, and berries.
They can live up to 24 years in the wild.

COW - A kine of cows
Cows are the most common farm animal in the world. They are raised for dairy and meat products and come in many colours.

F

FLYING SQUIRREL - A scurry of flying squirrels
There are more than 40 species of flying squirrels in the world. These squirrels don't actually fly, but glide from tree to tree - which looks like flying.

H

HONEY BEE - A swarm of honey bees
Honey bees are social creatures that live together in hives or nests. They produce the honey we eat and pollinate our flowers.

M

MOUSE - A mischief of mice
Mice are generally nocturnal rodents that have slender bodies and sharp claws.

MINNOW - A steam of minnows
Minnows are small freshwater fish found in North America. They are usually silver and measure less than four inches.

MOOSE - A herd of moose
Moose are large, herbivorous mammals that can live up to 15-20 years in the wild.

MOSQUITO - A scourge of mosquitoes
Only female mosquitoes bite humans and animals. Male mosquitoes feed on plants and only live for about a week.

N

NARWHAL - A blessing of narwhals
Narwhals are mammals that live in the Arctic. They are known as "the unicorn of the sea" because of their tusks.

O

ORCA - A pod of orcas
Orcas hunt together in groups and feed on fish, seals, walrus, penguins, sharks, and even other species of whales. They can live up to 80 years.

P

PEREGRINE FALCON - A cast of peregrine falcons
Peregrine falcons can be found in the tundra, desert, mountains, and even in cities. These carnivores can live up to 17 years.

POLAR BEAR - A celebration of polar bears
Polar bears live in the Arctic and are strong swimmers. They generally feed on seals. Their fur is white but their skin is black.

POLAR COD - A lap of polar cod
Polar cod live in the freezing cold water of the Arctic. They are the food source for narwhals, seals, and beluga whales.

PONY - A string of ponies
Ponies are small horses that come in many colours. They are a good breed for children to ride.

R

RACCOON - A gaze of raccoons
Raccoons are nocturnal mammals that live all over the world. They walk on four paws.

RED FOX - An earth of red fox
Red foxes are clever mammals. They generally hunt at night and eat rabbits, mice, snakes, and berries.

S

SEAL - A bob of seals
Seals are great swimmers and easily hunt for fish. They can live up to 20 years in the wild.

SALMON - A run of salmon
Salmon can live in both salt water and fresh water. These fish travel long distances to return to the place they were born to spawn.

SNOWY OWL - A parliament of snowy owls
Snowy owls mainly live in the Arctic tundra. Males are generally whiter than females, which are brownish with dark markings.

T

TOAD - A knot of toads
There are more than 300 different species of toads in the world. Toads have short legs compared to frogs.

W

WALRUS - A huddle of walrus
Walrus are large arctic mammals. They can live up to 40 years in the wild and have huge tusks.

Look and Match

a

b

c

d

e

f

g

h

i

j

k

l

m

n

o

p

q

r

s

t

u

v

w

x

y

z

aa

Write the letter on the line to match the animals to their names.

1. A polar bear   _____
2. A raccoon   _____
3. A snowy owl   _____
4. A beaver   _____
5. A walrus   _____
6. A honey bee   _____
7. An arctic hare   _____
8. A seal   _____
9. A bat   _____
10. A cow   _____
11. An orca   _____
12. A pony   _____
13. A butterfly   _____
14. A bass   _____

15. A salmon   _____
16. A minnow   _____
17. A mouse   _____
18. A mosquito   _____
19. A toad   _____
20. A peregrine falcon _____
21. A polar cod   _____
22. An arctic wolf   _____
23. A flying squirrel   _____
24. A moose   _____
25. A narwhal   _____
26. A red fox   _____
27. A Canada goose   _____

Quick quiz! Fill in the blanks with the animals from this book.

1. The _____ is known as the unicorn of the sea.

2. There are more than 300 species of _____ in the world.

3. _____ travel over 3,200 kilometres every year.

4. The most common farm animal in the world is the _____.

5. _____ can live up to 40 years in the wild.

Solutions

About the Authors

Caroline Fernandez is an award-winning author of children's books and blog posts. She is the author of *Stop Reading This Book*, *The Adventures of Grandmasaurus* (series), *Asha and Baz* (series), and more!

Twitter and Instagram: @ParentClub

www.parentclub.ca

Erin Mercer is an illustrator living in Nova Scotia with her husband and two cats. She has illustrated four other books for DC Canada Education Publishing, including *Recess in the Dark* and *Our Farm in the City*. She creates quirky greeting cards found in boutique gift shops across Canada and has worked in video game and animation studios.

Instagram: @pencilempire

www.pencilempire.com

9781772057997